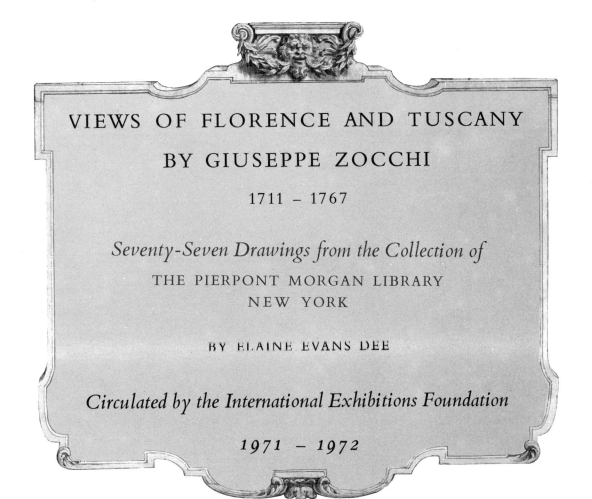

VIEWS OF FLORENCE AND TUSCANY

BY GIUSEPPE ZOCCHI

1711 – 1767

Seventy-Seven Drawings from the Collection of

THE PIERPONT MORGAN LIBRARY
NEW YORK

BY ELAINE EVANS DEE

Circulated by the International Exhibitions Foundation

1971 – 1972

LIST OF PARTICIPATING MUSEUMS

THE ART INSTITUTE OF CHICAGO
Chicago, Illinois

THE TOLEDO MUSEUM OF ART
Toledo, Ohio

WILLIAM ROCKHILL NELSON GALLERY
Kansas City, Missouri

THE SEATTLE ART MUSEUM
Seattle, Washington

PHOENIX ART MUSEUM
Phoenix, Arizona

TRUSTEES OF THE
INTERNATIONAL EXHIBITIONS FOUNDATION

PRODUCED BY THE MERIDEN GRAVURE COMPANY AND THE STINEHOUR PRESS

SECOND EDITION, 1971

ACKNOWLEDGEMENTS

THESE seventy-seven delightful drawings by Giuseppe Zocchi (1711–1767) from the collection of the Pierpont Morgan Library were originally shown there in the spring of 1968 and greatly admired by connoisseurs of Old Master drawings and the general public alike. The press, too, was enthusiastic; in the May, 1968, issue of *Apollo*, Mahonri Sharp Young wrote about "an unprecedented display of drawings by Giuseppe Zocchi, as a kind of Florentine salute," adding, "This is the most comprehensive record of Florentine monuments, street life, and surroundings in the eighteenth, or any other, century."

Very little is known about the artist, and the drawings were never exhibited until the Library decided to remove them from their albums and show them to the public for the first time together with the well-known engravings for which they are the final studies. The excellent photographs, also included in our exhibition, show the same views, villas, palaces, and churches as they are today. Taken by Elaine Evans Dee, these photographs document her intensive research on the artist and the buildings he portrayed in the middle of the eighteenth century. We wish to thank her for allowing us to publish her studies for the first time.

The Foundation arranged a short tour following the first New York showing and now, three years later, we are fortunate to send the drawings on a second tour. We are extremely grateful to Charles Ryskamp, Director of the Pierpont Morgan Library, and to the Trustees for the generous loan of the entire series of "Views." We also thank Felice Stampfle, Curator, Drawings and Prints, of the Library, for her wonderful cooperation throughout the years.

His Excellency Egidio Ortona, Ambassador of Italy, will sponsor the exhibition throughout its tour, and we wish to thank him for his unfailing interest in all projects of an artistic nature.

We look forward to the pleasure of sharing an exhibition of this rare quality and nostalgic beauty with our museum friends.

ANNEMARIE H. POPE
President
International Exhibitions Foundation

INTRODUCTION

IT has been said that the city of Florence, like Rome, has occupied itself most of all with the contemplation of its own historic beauty and the reception of visitors who come to do the same. To an American, particularly a New Yorker, resigned to the demolition and rebuilding which is a constant process in our cities, the homogeneity of Florentine buildings and the distinctly Renaissance character of the entire city is striking. The structures that still stand, the sculptures that still decorate them, and the paintings that still adorn their walls were for the most part placed there hundreds of years ago during the more than two centuries when Florence was the vital and creative core of the Renaissance cultural development.

View painting, which reached its apex during the eighteenth century, was a peculiarly Italian preoccupation. It stemmed from the same feelings of civic pride and sense of history that prompted the Italians to preserve older architecture. Added encouragement was given by the continuous influx of travelers who were potential customers for pictorial souvenirs. The eighteenth century was the great period of the Grand Tour, and Italy was considered to be its climax. The names of the view painters Guardi and Canaletto in Venice and Piranesi in Rome are familiar to everyone. Their contemporary in Florence, Giuseppe Zocchi, has been little known outside his native city until recently. The drawings in this exhibition represent the finished designs which Zocchi prepared for the engravings for two separate series of views: the *Scelta di XXIV vedute delle principali contrade, piazze, chiese, e palazzi della città di Firenze*, and the *Vedute delle ville e d'altri luoghi della Toscana*.

Both volumes were first published in 1744 and re-issued in 1754. Zocchi himself engraved two of the plates and the figures in five others; the remainder were parceled out to twenty-two different engravers. The designs were probably translated into prints by a process of making a tracing of the drawing onto a thinly varnished sheet of paper. This transparent sheet was then reversed on the plate and the design transferred, the final result being a print that did not reverse the drawing. The arrangement of the plates in both engraved volumes follows a logical geographical pattern, but the choice of views is not as understandable, particularly among the villas. It is puzzling, for instance, that the handsome "La Pietra" and the Villa Medici in Fiesole were omitted.

It is clear from the text of the title and dedicatory pages of the series that the specific purpose of the patron, the Marchese Andrea Gerini, in commissioning the work was to provide visitors with pictures to carry home. Gerini was a frequent visitor to Venice and was no doubt inspired by the wide production of *vedute* there. He chose his protégé of many years, Giuseppe Zocchi, to do the work. The facts concerning Zocchi's life are not plentiful. He was born near Florence in 1711, and died in 1767 of the plague which he had contracted in Siena. A painter as well as a draftsman, he was the official designer for the Pietre Dure (the so-called "Florentine mosaic") factory in Florence from 1754 to 1760. He had studied in Venice and in Bologna.

Zocchi's drawing style is less brilliant than Guardi's, not so lyrical as Canaletto's, and lacks the power of Piranesi's. Yet if studied closely with attention to detail, the drawings reveal an artist whose powers of observation were unsurpassed and whose skill as a draftsman was more than equal to his task. He did not always choose to be realistically precise; he seems to have had a passion for regularity and order which led him to adjust the Piazza Signoria from its distinctly irregular conformation to a neat square; he made level uneven building courses here and there; he opened vistas so that our view is complete and uninterrupted, and altered the perspective to suit his purposes. On the other hand, he was scrupulous in adhering to the correct propor-

tions within the architecture. Not only are the buildings of eighteenth-century Florence surveyed, but the people that moved in and about them as well. Humorous notes sound throughout—the poses of the innumerable sculptured and live dogs, the high spirited revelry of the costumed crowd at the *calcio* festival, and the occasional use of pure caricature. In the final analysis, the subject matter triumphs, for the drawings reflect clearly the life and the beauty of Florence and Tuscany as it existed in Zocchi's time.

The drawings and a copy of each of the volumes of engravings made after them came to the Pierpont Morgan Library in 1952 from the collection of Mrs. J. Pierpont Morgan as the gift of her sons. She had acquired them in England in the early years of the twentieth century. They had been bound in the eighteenth century, rebound in the nineteenth, and were unbound and exhibited individually for the first time in the spring of 1968 at the Library. Two additional drawings, also studies for engravings, of the feast of Santa Caterina de' Ricci at Prato were bound in the album but are not included in this catalogue.

Special thanks are due to my former colleagues at the Morgan Library who were helpful in a variety of ways in the preparation of the exhibition and catalogue, to Professors Howard Saalman, Webster Smith, and Rudolf Wittkower, and to all those Florentines who graciously welcomed me and contributed freely of their knowledge and time.

ELAINE EVANS DEE
Cooper-Hewitt Museum, New York
Smithsonian Institution

CATALOGUE

The number in parenthesis following the title indicates the plate number of the related engraving (F for the Florentine views, V for the villas).

Each of the views of Florence is drawn on paper containing the watermark, or some fragment of it, of a fleur-de-lis in a shield surmounted by a crown (Heawood 1803: Amsterdam, 1721). As the villas are drawn on half-sheets, the watermarks occur only where indicated. The inscriptions identifying the subjects are all on the mounts, in pen and brown ink. Each of the villas is numbered on the verso (visible through the mount).

The text illustrations are taken from the group of modern photographs annotating the exhibition.

1. DEDICATORY PAGE

Pen and black ink, and gray wash. 19⅛ × 12⅛ inches (485 × 307 mm.) The artist has corrected the drawing by adding paper over the face of the figure at the right.

Inscribed in pen and black ink beneath the medallion: *MARIA. THERESIA | PIA. FELIX | AUGUSTA.* The long dedication in pen and brown ink is dated *Firenze primo Luglio MDCCXLIV* and signed *Andrea Gerini.*

The gracious dedication to Maria Theresa states the purpose of the series by its sponsor, Andrea Gerini. The Marchese Gerini was a Florentine collector and Zocchi's patron. The aim of the commission was to provide "curious spectators, and especially strangers, noble and handsome views of the principal streets, squares, churches, and palaces" of the city. The date of the inscription coincides with the publication of the first edition of the engravings.

2. TITLE PAGE: VIEWS OF FLORENCE

Black chalk. 18⅜ × 26⅝ inches (467 × 676 mm.) Inscribed in pen and brown ink on the pedestal in center: *Scelta | di XXIV. Vedute delle principali | Contrade, Piazze, Chiese, e Palazzi, della Città di Firenze | Dedicata | Alla Sacra Reale Apostolica | Maesta di | Maria Teresa | Regina d'Ingheria | e di Boemia, | Arciduchessa d'Austria | e Granduchessa | di Toscana &c. &c. &c.;* on a cartouche below: *Questo Frontespizio dato ora in luce per la prima volta, è preso | dalla Pittura originale à fresco fatta dal Mannozzi detto Giovanni | da San Giovanni nel Prospetto di una Casa posta in Firenze in faccia | alla Porta Romana.*

The title page for the series is not the work of Zocchi, but of Giuseppi Magni. As the inscription informs us, it is based on a fresco by Giovanni da San Giovanni (1596–1636) on the exterior wall of a house opposite the Porta Romana. The subject is an allegorical representation of the city of Florence. Andrea Gerini commissioned the copy in order to preserve through the engraving the composition of the already disintegrating fresco.

1. DEDICATORY PAGE

dral, the tower of the Palazzo Vecchio, San Lorenzo, the Pitti Palace, Santo Spirito, and San Frediano in Cestello, among others. The wall was constructed from 1284 to 1333 and was the third to be built around the city. Projecting from it at the right is the Fortezza da Basso, a Renaissance fort still remarkably well preserved, where the splendid conservation laboratories constructed after the 1966 flood are now located.

It would appear from the group at the left that in this instance the patron, Andrea Gerini, actively directed the artist in his depiction of the sights below them.

3. VIEW OF FLORENCE FROM THE CAPUCHIN MONASTERY IN MONTUGHI (F.1)

Pen and black ink, and gray wash. 18½ × 26 9/16 inches (470 × 676 mm.) Signed in pen and black ink at lower left with the monogram *GZ*; inscribed on the mount in pen and brown ink: *Veduta di Firenze dal Convento de' P. P. Cappuccini di Montughi.*

Florence can be seen from so many fine vantage points from the surrounding hills that it is difficult to decide which is the loveliest. Zocchi chose the Montughi section to the north. The drawing reads like a guidebook to the city; from left to right one can identify the major monuments—the Cathe-

4. THE PITTI PALACE (F.2)

Pen and black ink, and gray wash. 18⅜ × 26⅜ inches (466 × 670 mm.) Inscribed: *Veduta del Reale Palazzo de Pitti Abitazione de Regnanti Sovrani.*

Begun in 1457 for Luca Pitti, a rival of the Medici, the imposing cubic structure faced with chiseled masonry was built under the direction of the architect Luca Fancelli. An Elizabethan traveler (Henry Wotton) found it "the most magnificent and regular pile within the Christian world." In 1549, the Pitti family sold the palace to Eleanor of Toledo, wife of Duke Cosimo I Medici, and the creation of the Boboli Gardens behind the palace began. Extensions and alterations continued to be made to the already grandiose building until about 1765, when the final annexes to the front wings were added. The palace was the residence of the Italian royal family until the establishment of the Republic in 1946. It now houses five separate museums, and the Boboli Gardens are open to visitors. As in the eighteenth century, the piazza serves as a parking lot for the palace.

5. VIEW ALONG THE ARNO RIVER FROM THE PORTA ALLA CROCE (F.3)

Pen and black ink, and gray wash. 18⅜ × 26¾ inches (467 × 680 mm.)
Inscribed: *Veduta di una parte di Firenze presa fuori della Porta alla Croce presso al Fiume Arno.*

Although the Florentines have had many occasions to echo Dante's description of the Arno River as the "cursed and unlucky ditch," it has played a dominant role in the economy and history of the city. Zocchi included six views in this series along its two-mile course through Florence, the first showing the southern bank (the Oltrarno) at the eastern edge of the city. The Porta alla Croce is several hundred yards north of the river at this point. At the left of the drawing is the fortified gate of the Porta a San Niccolò, built about 1323 and demolished in 1870, except for the tower, for a new street. Just to the right of the tower, on the hill beyond, is the long, narrow palace, called *La Palazzina*, inside the Belvedere fortress which occupies a corner of the Boboli Gardens.

The four-story Palazzo Torrigani, its open loggia at the top, overlooks the Ponte alle Grazie which was for centuries the longest and oldest bridge in Florence. It withstood the great flood of 1333, only to be destroyed by German mines in 1944. (It has since been reconstructed.) The small houses on the bridge in the drawing were occupied by hermit nuns as penitence, or served as chapels; they were removed at the end of the nineteenth century. The fishermen in the foreground are in a dammed area called *La Pescaia*, still a favorite spot among anglers.

6. VIEW ALONG THE ARNO RIVER FROM THE PORTA A SAN NICCOLÒ (F.4)

Pen and black ink. 18⅜ × 26½ inches (466 × 675 mm.)
Inscribed: *Veduta di una parte di Firenze presa fuori della Porta à S. Niccolò presso al Fiume Arno.*

Now slightly further upstream and facing in the opposite direction, the artist is looking at the north bank of the Arno. The building with the square tower at the far right was the Zecca Vecchia (Old Mint), probably established here in the 1380's. It is now destroyed, along with all the other buildings at the river's edge shown in this drawing, for the Lungarno della Zecca Vecchia. Behind the riverfront buildings can be seen the familiar forms of the Cathedral and its campanile, the apse of Santa Croce, the upper section of Orsanmichele, and the Palazzo Vecchio. The Ponte Vecchio is just visible beyond the Ponte alle Grazie.

Although the genre scenes in all the drawings reveal in considerable detail the character of life at every level in eighteenth-century Florence, in the river scenes Zocchi seems to become even more intimate and personal in his descriptions. He catalogues a whole range of river craft, from barges for freight to pleasure boats with striped awnings. An atmosphere of relaxed nonchalance prevails. The drawing style in the delineation of the figures is particularly broad and free.

7. VIEW ALONG THE ARNO RIVER FROM THE VAGA LOGGIA (F.5)

Pen and black ink over preliminary indications in black chalk.
18⅝ × 26⅝ inches (472 × 677 mm.)
Inscribed: *Veduta d'una parte di Firenze presa dalla Vaga Loggia.*

This drawing of the river is made from the opposite edge of the city, from the city walls on the west, looking towards the south bank. The artist, who appears again with a gesticulating companion, took a viewpoint near the mill, the

Mulina della Vagaloggia. It had been erected in the fourteenth century, but was razed in 1854 for the construction of the Lungarno Vespucci. The spillway across the river is all that remains. The church of San Frediano in Cestello at the far right was begun in 1680 by the Roman architect Cerutti. It looks much the same today, its façade still unfinished. In the center of the drawing are the campanile and church of Santo Spirito; in the distance beyond them one has another glimpse of the Forte Belvedere.

The bridge is the Ponte alla Carraia, first built in 1218–20 and called the Ponte Nuovo to distinguish it from the Ponte Vecchio. It suffered numerous disasters, once collapsing under the weight of a crowd watching a pageant of Hell being performed on the river. It was completely destroyed by the German army in 1945, but has since been rebuilt.

8. THE ARNO RIVER AND THE PONTE SANTA TRINITA (F.6)

Pen and black ink, some brown ink and gray wash over preliminary indications in black chalk. $18\frac{3}{4} \times 26\frac{11}{16}$ inches (475 × 681 mm.)
Inscribed: *Veduta di una parte di Lung'Arno, e del Ponte à S. Trinita, presa dal Palazzo del Sig:ᵣ March. Ruberto Capponi.*

The graceful elliptical arches of the Ponte Santa Trinita support one of the busiest thoroughfares in Florence. The bridge was designed by Bartolomeo Ammanati and built between 1567 and 1570. According to Vasari, Michelangelo had made notes and drawings for this project, but there is no proof that Ammanati based his design on Michelangelo's. During World War II, Ponte Santa Trinita was blown up, but it was completely rebuilt following Ammanati's original designs which had fortunately been preserved. Even some of the sixteenth-century stones were retrieved from

the river. The statues flanking the bridge at either end represent the Seasons and were placed there in 1608 to celebrate the marriage of Cosimo II to Maddalena of Austria. The buildings across the river to the left of the bridge belonged in Zocchi's time to the Gianfigliazzi family, as they had since the Middle Ages; the palace to the right of the bridge was the Palazzo Spini. The view was taken from what is now the Lungarno Guicciardini in front of the palace belonging to the Capponi, another prominent Florentine family, and the building at the end of the bridge with the highly ornamented window and door frames is the Palazzo Frescobaldi.

The Ponte Vecchio, which is also visible, is the oldest bridge in Florence, dating from Roman times. The present bridge was finished in 1345. The existence of shops on the bridge has been recorded since the end of the thirteenth century. Originally, they were butchers' stalls, but in 1593 Ferdinando I leased them instead to the gold and silversmiths, who still largely occupy them today. The 1966 floods swept away some of the shops and much of their contents.

9. THE ARNO RIVER FROM THE RUCELLAI TERRACE (F.7)

Pen and black ink, and gray wash. $18\frac{3}{8} \times 26\frac{1}{2}$ inches (465 × 673 mm.)
Inscribed: *Veduta di Lung'Arno e del Ponte à S. Trinita, presa dal Terrazzo de SS.ʳⁱ Rucellai.*

The artist's viewpoint in this drawing is across the river and downstream from that of the previous drawing; what in his time was called the Rucellai Terrace is now part of the Lungarno Corsini. The view encompasses the buildings on both sides of the river between the Ponte Santa Trinita and the

Ponte alla Carraia. On the south bank, the scene is dominated by the dome and campanile of Santo Spirito. The church was designed by Brunelleschi, but built after his death; the dome was erected in the last decade of the fifteenth century after designs by Giuliano da Sangallo and perhaps by Antonio del Pollaiuolo, except for the lantern which is seventeenth century. The campanile, although begun in 1490, was not finished until 1571. Along the river front below are various sixteenth-century palaces, ending at the bridge with the Capponi. In the far distance can be discerned the Romanesque church and Bishop's palace of San Miniato al Monte (strangely enough its only appearance in the series), with the Palazzina to the right and the fifteenth-century church of San Salvatore al Monte to the left of it. The buildings on the north bank shown in profile are treated in greater detail in catalogue nos. 8 and 10.

The genre scenes in this drawing are particularly appealing: the ballad singer with his attentive audience, the pipe-smoking boatman, and the pair leaning on the wall engaged in lively conversation.

10. THE CORSINI PALACE ON THE ARNO RIVER (F.8)

Pen and black ink, and gray wash. $18\frac{1}{2} \times 26\frac{3}{4}$ inches (470×678 mm.) Inscribed: *Veduta di una parte di Lung'Arno dalla parte opposta al Palazzo del Sig:*^{re} *P.*^e *Corsini.*

The grand palace which occupies the major part of the right half of the drawing is the Corsini, a rare example of the baroque style in Florence. It represents the result of the remodeling (1648–56) of older structures purchased or inherited by the Marchese Filippo Corsini and his wife, Maria

Machiavelli. To the left of it on the corner of the Piazza Goldoni is the Palazzo Ricasoli. Its exterior murals, painted in the 1550's by Francesco Pagani, have now weathered away, but they can be seen in Zocchi's drawing in the upper stories between the windows.

The extensive Corsini collection of painting and sculpture housed in the palace is now open to the public.

11. THE CHURCH AND PIAZZA OGNISSANTI (F.9)

Pen and black ink, and gray wash. $18\frac{5}{16} \times 26\frac{3}{8}$ inches (465×665 mm.) Inscribed: *Veduta della Chiesa, e Piazza d'Ognissanti.*

The Piazza Ognissanti is on the north bank of the river

downstream from the Ponte Carraia. Facing the river, on the piazza, is the church. It was originally built in 1256 and its campanile, which resembles that of Santa Maria Novella, was erected about fifty years later. A series of alterations in the sixteenth and seventeenth centuries changed the looks of the building completely, the façade by Matteo Nigetti of 1637 being one of the first examples of baroque church architecture in Florence.

At the left of the piazza in the drawing is the Palazzo Lenzi-Quaratesi, a mid-fifteenth-century building. The building across from it was rebuilt in 1835 as the Palazzo Bonaparte. Deluxe hotels now occupy the piazza, and the hustle and bustle of automobiles has replaced the make-shift seesaw Zocchi included as part of the scene. The artist seems also to have taken considerable liberties with the scale in the drawing, as the piazza is not nearly so deep as it appears to be here.

12. THE STROZZI PALACE, THE *CENTAURO*, AND THE STREET LEADING TO SANTA MARIA NOVELLA (F.10)
Pen and black ink, and gray wash. 18 7/16 × 26 1/2 inches (467 × 670 mm.)
Inscribed: *Veduta del Palazzo del Sig:*ʳᵉ *March:*ˢᵉ *Strozzi, del Centauro, e della Strada, che conduce à S. Maria Novella.*

The Via Cerretani which begins at the Piazza del Duomo divides into three branches where the sculptured group stands in the drawing, the central branch leading into the Piazza Santa Maria Novella. The sculpture is Giovanni da Bologna's *Hercules and the Centaur* which was placed on this site in 1600 and, after several moves, finally in the nineteenth century found a permanent home on the Loggia de' Lanzi.

The Strozzi Palace at the left, built in 1720, is popularly known as the Palazzo delle Cento Finestre (Palace of One Hundred Windows), and also as the Palazzo Franchetti. Most of the houses in the row at the right have been remodeled.

13. CHURCH OF SAN MICHELE BERTELDE (F.11)
Pen and black ink, and gray wash. 18 5/16 × 26 1/4 inches (465 × 667 mm.)
Inscribed: *Veduta della Chiesa de S. Michele Bertelde de' P.P. Teatini.*

The church, now known as San Gaetano, was established originally in 1055. In 1592, the Theatine order acquired the site and instituted a fifty-year building program, completely changing the character of the building, under the direction of the architects Matteo Nigetti and Gherardo Silvani and his son. The sculptural decoration of the façade is late seventeenth-century. When the Theatines were expelled a century later, San Michele became a parish church.

The square on which the church stands is named after the Palazzo Antinori, the rusticated fifteenth-century palace on the left, possibly designed by Giuliano da Sangallo. The Via Tornabuoni begins in this piazza and leads to the Ponte Santa Trinita.

14. THE CORSI AND VIVIANI PALACES (F.12)
Pen and black ink, and gray wash. 18 3/8 × 26 1/2 inches (467 × 673 mm.)
Inscribed: *Veduta de' Palazzi de' Sig: March. Corsi, e Viviani.*

In Zocchi's time as one walked along the Via Tornabuoni towards the river to the intersection of the Via Strozzi, and turned to look back, the view was dominated by the palace of the Marchese Corsi on the right and the Palazzo Viviani on the left. The Palazzo Corsi occupied the entire block between the Via Strozzi in the right foreground, and the church of San Gaetano. It was completely rebuilt in 1875 as part of an extensive renovation project of the Via Tornabuoni, the final chapter in a long history of construction and alteration. Of the original fifteenth-century palace, built by Michelozzo for the Tornabuoni family, only the courtyard remains; the building is now occupied by a bank.

The Palazzo Viviani across the street was redesigned by Giovanni Battista Foggini in 1693, incorporating several earlier buildings. The rusticated arches on the ground floor may well have always opened into shops, as they do today. The slender corner of the seventeenth-century Palazzo Dudley is at the extreme left of the drawing; its colorful owner also owned one of the villas outside Florence which Zocchi drew (catalogue no. 57).

15. THE STROZZI PALACE AND THE STREET LEADING TO THE PONTE SANTA TRINITA (F.13)

Pen and black ink, and gray wash. 18⅜ × 26½ inches (467 × 673 mm.)
Inscribed: *Veduta del Palazzo del Sig:re Principe Strozzi, e della Strada, che conduce al Ponte à S. Trinita.*

Making an about-face from the viewpoint of the previous drawing, with a corner of the Palazzo Dudley now at the right, we see in the foreground the magnificent Renaissance palace begun in 1489 for Filippo Strozzi. The names of several designers and architects have been associated with the palace: Benedetto da Maiano, Giuliano da Sangallo, and Cronaca. The fine wrought-iron lanterns, torch holders, and

rings on the ground floor were made by Niccolò Grosso Caparra about 1500. The construction of the building extended well into the sixteenth century; the rear of the palace and the cornice remained incomplete until it was restored in 1938.

The buildings at the end of the Via Tornabuoni are dealt with in detail in the following drawing; the houses on both sides of the street in the middle of the block were rebuilt in the nineteenth century.

16. THE PIAZZA SANTA TRINITA (F.14)

Pen and black ink, and gray wash over preliminary indications in black chalk. 18 7/16 × 26 9/16 inches (468 × 674 mm.)
Inscribed: *Veduta del Ponte a S. Trinita, della Chiesa di S. Trinita, e della Colonna inalzata da Cosimo I.*

The column of oriental granite which supports the figure of Justice by Francesco del Tadda was a gift to Cosimo I by Pope Pius IV. Cosimo erected the column in the center of the piazza in 1560 to commemorate a military triumph. Baccio d'Agnolo was the architect of the Palazzo Bartolini at the far left (built about 1520 and restored in 1962). Next to it is the Palazzo Buondelmonti, a thirteenth-century structure renovated in the early sixteenth century. The large, medieval Palazzo Spini (now Ferroni) behind the column is seen in this drawing from still another angle. From the thirteenth century until 1823 when it was recessed for fear of its collapsing, the river side of the palace rose from the bed of the Arno, and a vaulted passageway under the palace allowed the movement of traffic along the riverbank.

A seventeenth-century historian recorded that the church of Santa Trinita was one of the twelve collegiate churches founded by Charlemagne in 810. The present church is the result of numerous building programs on the original site, but by about 1405 most of the church was finished, the one remaining major addition to the existing church being the impressive exterior façade designed by Bernardo Buontalenti in 1592.

17. THE PIAZZA SANTISSIMA ANNUNZIATA (F.15)

Pen and black ink, and gray wash over preliminary indications in black chalk. 18½ × 26⅝ inches (468 × 675 mm.)
Inscribed: *Veduta della Piazza della SS. Nunziata, Statua Equestre di Ferdinando Primo, Fonti, e Loggie Laterali.*

The list of names of illustrious artists and architects associated with this piazza and the buildings on it reads like a textbook of Florentine art. The remodeling of the medieval structure of the church of Santissima Annunziata and its massive monastery alongside was begun by Michelozzo and continued by Leone Battista Alberti and Antonio Manetti. Andrea del Sarto, Jacopo Pontormo, and Rosso Fiorentino contributed to the frescoes which ornament the atrium. The loggia at the right, in shadow, is that of the Ospedale degli Innocenti designed by Filippo Brunelleschi and adorned with the beloved glazed terra-cotta medallions of swaddled infants by Andrea della Robbia. On the opposite side of the piazza, Antonio da Sangallo and Baccio d'Agnolo built the loggia of the Confraternity of the Servi di Maria to reflect the style of Brunelleschi's foundling hospital.

Giovanni da Bologna is responsible for the monument of Ferdinand I in the center (inspired by the equestrian statue of Marcus Aurelius on the Capitoline Hill in Rome), and the fountains on either side are the work of Pietro Tacca.

18. THE HOSPITAL AND PIAZZA OF SANTA MARIA NUOVA (F.16)

Pen and black ink, and gray wash. 18⅜ × 26⅜ inches (466 × 671 mm.)
Inscribed: *Veduta dello Spedale, e della Piazza di S. Maria Nuova.*

The portico which renders this piazza one of the most beautiful in Florence was designed by Bernardo Buontalenti. The construction of the loggia progressed at slow and infrequent intervals: the first campaign took place 1612–16 under the direction of Giulio Parigi, the second 1661–63, the third 1707–10, and a three-arched projecting arm, corresponding to that on the right in the drawing, was finished only in 1960. The hospital was founded by Folco Portinari (the father of Dante's Beatrice) about 1286, adjacent to the church of San Egidio. The main entrance to both is through the loggia.

19. CHURCH AND PIAZZA SAN PIER MAGGIORE (F.17)

Pen and black ink, and gray wash. 18⅜ × 24¼ inches (466 × 668 mm.)
Inscribed: *Veduta della Chiesa, e Piazza di S. Pier Maggiore.*

An Early Christian church first occupied this location; it was remodeled in the eleventh century, and rebuilt in the fourteenth with a campanile similar to that of Santa Maria Novella. Further alterations and additions were made in subsequent periods, including the three-arched portico by Matteo Nigetti in 1638 and the upper portion of the façade some years later. In 1783, one of the Gothic arches of the nave collapsed and the church was torn down. Today only the arcaded portico remains; its central arch has become a passageway, shops occupy the side arches, and the upper section has been converted to living quarters. The Renaissance palace with the rusticated lower story at the left of the drawing is the Palazzo Albizzi.

south, the apse facing the piazza. The shops built into the church behind the apse still exist, but the double-ramped stair to the main portal, through which one entered the side of the church, does not.

The Palazzo del Podestà, or Bargello as it is more popularly called, is the earliest civic building in Florence. The Podestà was an elected official in charge of the administration of justice, a severe example of which is taking place in the drawing. The original palace of 1250 underwent innumerable changes and additions throughout the centuries until the middle of the nineteenth, when the prisons which occupied part of it were removed and the National Museum of Sculpture was located here. The wrought-iron lion on top of the great tower dates from the fourteenth century.

A complex structure known as San Firenze, which houses the tribunal and two separate churches, is on the site of the oratory to which Zocchi refers in the title.

20. THE BADIA FIORENTINA AND THE PALAZZO DEL PODESTÀ (F.18)

Pen and black ink, and gray wash over preliminary indications in black chalk. 18 7/16 × 26 7/16 inches (469 × 671 mm.)
Inscribed: *Veduta della Badia Fiorentina, e del Palazzo del Potestà, presa dalla Piazza della Chiesa de PP. dell' Oratorio.*

The church of the Badia occupies one side of the triangular Piazza San Firenze. In 1825, the tenth-century Benedictine abbey was replaced by a large Gothic structure, with its altar end oriented east in the traditional manner, the rear wall facing the street just off the piazza. In the seventeenth century, the three-aisled building was transformed into the Renaissance form of a Greek cross, and re-oriented north to

21. THE CHURCH OF SAN GIOVANNINO AND THE RICCARDI PALACE (F.19)

Pen and black ink, and gray wash. 18 1/4 × 26 7/16 inches (465 × 670 mm.) The artist has corrected the drawing by adding paper over the upper story of the palace.
Inscribed: *Veduta della Piazza, e Chiesa di S: Giovannino de PP: Gesuiti, e de Palazzi dei SS:ri March:e Riccardi, e Panciatichi.*

San Giovanni Evangelista, or San Giovannino degli Scolopi, was the headquarters of the Jesuits in Florence until the order was suppressed by the Pope in 1773. The church and its adjoining college were then given to the Padri Scolopi, another teaching order. The building was begun in the sixteenth and finished in the seventeenth century after plans by Ammanati. The Riccardi Palace was the first great family palace of the Renaissance, built for Cosimo de' Medici by Michelozzo, 1444–60. The palace chapel contains Benozzo Gozzoli's famous frescoes of the *Journey of the Magi.* About 1517, Michelangelo filled in the arches at the corner, originally the entrance to a loggia. After its acquisition by the Riccardi family in 1659, the structure was expanded further. It now houses the Medici Museum. Only a corner of the Panciatichi Palace across the Via Cavour shows in the drawing; it dates from about 1700.

22. THE UFFIZI FROM THE LOGGIA NEAR THE ARNO RIVER (F.20)

Pen and black ink, and gray wash. 18 7/16 × 26 9/16 inches (468 × 674 mm.)
Inscribed: *Veduta degli Ufizi, ò sia Curia Fiorentina, presa dalla Loggia presso Arno.*

Zocchi's dramatic view of the Uffizi permits us to look through the two long wings of the building to the Palazzo Vecchio and the Piazza della Signoria. He stretched the vista at the end of the perspective to include the cupola of the Cathedral. The Uffizi was designed by Giorgio Vasari for Cosimo I in 1560, and the project was continued by Buontalenti after Vasari's death in 1574. The primary purpose of the edifice was to house the thirteen principal magistrates of the duchy and their staffs. An elevated corridor was constructed over the Ponte Vecchio connecting the Uffizi with the Pitti Palace to keep the ruler in close contact with his deputies. By 1581, the Uffizi was already functioning as a gallery to display the Medici treasures, which it continues to do today on a vastly expanded scale. The niches along the court, empty in Zocchi's time, were filled during the nineteenth century with sculptured portraits of illustrious Florentines.

23. THE CATHEDRAL AND BAPTISTERY DURING THE PROCESSION OF CORPUS DOMINI (F.21)

Pen and black ink, and gray wash. 18 1/2 × 26 5/8 inches (471 × 675 mm.)
Inscribed: *Veduta della Metropolitana Fiorentina, e del Battistero di S. Gio. con La Processione del Corpus Domini.*

The religious life of the city centers around the Cathedral (Santa Maria del Fiore). Zocchi's view, which encompasses a wider sweep than would be possible from any one vantage point, shows the magnificent building with its pink, dark green, and white marbles from the north. In fact, so large is the Cathedral that there is no spot on the piazza from which all of it can be seen at once. Arnolfo di Cambio contributed the first design for the Cathedral in the late thirteenth century; Giotto was appointed to build the campanile in 1334; and by 1436 Brunelleschi had completed the dome and designed the lantern which Michelozzo finished. The façade remained bare of facing until 1875–87; that shown in the drawing was painted on the front of the church. San Giovanni, for whom the Baptistery and the piazza are named, is the patron saint of the city. The Baptistery is a Romanesque remodeling (finished 1150) of an earlier structure. Its famous bronze doors were not made until the fourteenth and fifteenth centuries.

The feast of Corpus Domini was celebrated each year on June 23, in connection with the feast of San Giovanni. The saint's relics were carried under a canopy from the Cathedral to the Baptistery, and after a long procession through the city, back to the Cathedral.

24. THE CHURCH AND PIAZZA OF SANTA MARIA NOVELLA DURING THE CHARIOT RACE (F.22)

Pen and black ink, and gray wash over preliminary indications in black chalk. $18^5/_8 \times 26^1/_2$ inches (472 × 675 mm.)
Inscribed: *Veduta della Chiesa, e Piazza di S. Maria Novella con la Festa della Corsa de' Cocchi.*

The present church of Santa Maria Novella was begun in 1246 by the Dominicans on land then outside the city walls. It was completed in the thirteenth century except for the façade which was finished by Alberti in the fifteenth. During this period the church was considered the center of religious orthodoxy and political conservatism in the city. The recessed niches in the façade and in the wall of the cemetery to the right contain the tombs of wealthy families. Brunelleschi's Ospedale degli Innocenti was the model for the hospital complex of San Paolo de' Convalescenti across the piazza.

The chariot race, initiated by Cosimo I in 1563, took place annually on the eve of the feast of San Giovanni. Four chariots making three laps around the piazza competed for the prize. The obelisks which marked the course became permanent fixtures of the piazza in 1608, when they were made by Giovanni da Bologna.

25. THE PIAZZA DELLA SIGNORIA DURING THE FESTIVAL OF HOMAGE (F.23)

Pen and black ink, and gray wash. $18^9/_{16} \times 26^3/_4$ inches (472 × 680 mm.)
Inscribed: *Veduta del Palazzo Vecchio del G. D., della Loggia, e della Piazza, con la Festa degli Omaggi nella Solennità di S. Gio. Batista Protettore della Città.*

Along with the Cathedral square and the modern Piazza della Repubblica, the Piazza della Signoria is one of the three main squares of the city. It takes its name from the Palazzo Vecchio, also called the Palazzo della Signoria, which from about 1300 was the meeting place for the officers of Florence. The building grew in irregular fashion incorporating other palaces. In Stendhal's words, "this stark, contrasting incarnation of the stern realities of mediaeval times set square amid the artistic glories of the past . . . creates an impression of unparalleled grandeur and truth." Regardless of the form of government of the city, the Palazzo has been its headquarters; it is still serving as the city hall. Beyond the Palazzo is the fourteenth-century Loggia de' Lanzi, named for the Swiss lancers of Cosimo I. It was built to provide an open-air sculpture gallery and a protected place for public ceremonies, as in the occasion depicted here of the offering of vassalage, indicated by the lowering of a banner in token of respect before the sovereign seated on the Loggia. At the far corner of the piazza is a glimpse of the Uffizi, and most of the sculpture which ornaments the piazza is still in place today.

26. THE CHURCH AND PIAZZA OF SANTA CROCE (F.24)

Pen and black ink, and gray wash over preliminary indications in black chalk. $18^3/_8 \times 26^1/_2$ inches (467 × 673 mm.)
Inscribed: *Veduta della Chiesa, e Piazza di S. Croce con La Festa del Calcio fatta L'anno 1738 alla Real presenza de Regnanti Sovrani.*

The Church of Santa Croce was founded by the Franciscans about 1295. Although the building was more or less finished by the fourteenth century, the façade of rough stone was as yet unadorned in the eighteenth century; in fact, the polychrome marble facing was not finally applied until 1854–63. The church was built on a grand scale, and due to the patronage of the commune and rich mercantile families, its beautiful chapter-room, chapels, and cloister, as well as its sculpture and murals, are unrivaled. In spite of the particularly damaging effects of the 1966 flood, much of the square is as Zocchi drew it.

The traditional soccer game (*calcio*) was more of a display than a contest. It was an opportunity for the Florentine nobility to present themselves in elaborate costumes—all the characters from the Commedia dell'Arte can be seen in the foreground of the drawing. As for the game, about twenty-five players on each side participated, striving to propel by foot and fist a large inflated ball into the opponent's pavilion.

Villas and Views of Tuscany

27. TITLE PAGE: VIEWS OF VILLAS AND SITES IN TUSCANY
Pen and black ink, and gray wash over preliminary indications in black chalk. 12 3/16 × 18 3/4 inches (310 × 475 mm.)
Signed, upside down, in pen and black ink on a scroll at lower right: *Giuseppe Zocchi delin | et inventor*; inscribed on a pedestal at center: *VEDUTE | DI VILLE, E LUOGHI | DELLA TOSCANA | AN. MDCCXXXXIV*

The artist has extended every possible courtesy on the opening page of the series of villas; he bows to Florence and Tuscany, the reigning monarchs, his patron, and himself. The mythological figures at the left suggest the production of the land and the commerce on which Florence and Tuscany thrived. Maria Theresa of Austria, the Grand Duchess of Tuscany, gestures towards the patron of the book, Andrea Gerini, whose bust stands on a pedestal bearing his coat of arms. Beyond the bust, one putto, alluding to what is about to come, exhorts another to draw the three Gerini villas in the distance. Below the medallion containing Zocchi's self-portrait are the tools of his trade, and a sly reference to the

Florentine series by means of the page, showing the Cathedral, draped casually over the step

28. VILLA POGGIO IMPERIALE (v.1)
Pen and black ink, and gray wash. 11 × 18 7/8 inches (280 × 480 mm.)
Watermark
Inscribed: *La Real Villa, detta il Poggio Imperiale.*

The villa stands enthroned in the center of its circular yard at the end of a wide boulevard which begins at the Porta Romana, the southernmost gate of the city. Constructed on the site of an ancient castle, it passed through the hands of many prominent Florentine families before it was acquired for the Grand Duchess Maria Maddalena of the imperial family of Austria, wife of Cosimo II de' Medici, for whom it was titled "imperial." About 1620, she commissioned Giulio Parigi to enlarge the villa. From that time it became a favorite residence of the Medici princes. Zocchi's drawing records the Parigi façade which was completely altered in the nineteenth century to conform to neo-classic taste. The circular wall has been rebuilt, retaining the sculptures of Jupiter and Atlas by Vincenzo de' Rossi (1563) at the entrance. Since 1864, Poggio Imperiale has been a school for girls.

29. LA PACE (v.2)
Pen and black ink, and gray wash over preliminary indications in black chalk. 11 1/16 × 18 7/8 inches (281 × 480 mm.) Watermark
Inscribed: *La Pace.*

Santa Maria della Pace was located near the Porta Romana. It had originated in the sixteenth century, but by Zocchi's time, numerous structural revisions had been made, among them the closing in of the arcades along the sides, the intrusion of two doors in the front to gain access to the newly created aisles, the addition of buttressing to the upper story of the nave, and the elaboration of the exterior ornament. The convent behind it was also expanded considerably in the eighteenth century. The church no longer exists, probably sacrificed to the construction of boulevards in the twentieth century.

30. VILLA RICCI AT POZZOLATICO (v.3)

Pen and black ink, and gray wash. 11 × 18⅞ inches (279 × 478 mm.)
Inscribed: *Pozzolatico Villa del Sig:ʳ Senat:ʳᵉ Ricci.*

The Villa Ricci is located due south of Florence in the village of Pozzolatico, overlooking the super-highway which by-passes Florence on the route to Bologna. The villa was owned by the Ricci family in the fourteenth century, and is most usually called the Villa Larderel, but its most celebrated tenant was the beautiful Countess Mirafiori whose morganatic marriage to Victor Emmanuel II took place in 1869 in the chapel of the villa. The eighteenth-century appearance is little changed today except for the loss of the central pediment, and the fact that the building is part of a modern complex of structures that has most recently been used as a school.

31. VILLA I COLLAZZI (v.4)

Pen and black ink. 11 × 18⅝ inches (280 × 472 mm.)
Inscribed: *Villa de Collazzi de SS:ʳⁱ Dini.*

For many years, Michelangelo was considered to be the architect of this villa, but it is now given to Santo di Tito. Michelangelo was a friend of Augustino Dini, for whom

the villa was built; in 1560 when it was begun, Michelangelo was working in Florence, and the simple, harmonious design and stately grandeur of the villa and its gardens seem in keeping with his style. In the nineteenth century, the villa was owned by Bombicci-Pomi; it is sometimes called by this name. When the present owners acquired it in 1933, in spite of past efforts it was still unfinished, looking rather as it did on the savagely windy day Zocchi drew it. At long last, however, the left wing matches the right, and the garden façade has been completed. The villa lies in the midst of undulating hills a few miles south of Florence.

32. CASTLE OF MONTEGUFONI (v.5)

Pen and black ink. 11 × 18⅝ inches (280 × 472 mm.) The artist has corrected the drawing by adding paper over the trees at the lower left.
Inscribed: *Villa di Monte Gufoni delli SS:ʳⁱ March:ˢⁱ Acciaioli.*

The first glimpse of Montegufoni is through the pale green mist of olive groves from the road ascending southeast towards Montespertoli. It was built in the thirteenth century by the Cardinal Acciaiuoli as a fortress villa and as a means of displaying his power and magnificence. Subsequent generations of occupants have changed its form, and it has acquired a baroque façade. The tower remains, and none of its alterations have detracted from its romantic character. Sir Osbert Sitwell, the present owner, has described it in his autobiography: ". . . it exhaled an air of remote and true rusticity, as well as wafting across the centuries the breath of a grandeur belonging to a legendary past . . . . Each year, with the opening up of courts and rooms, Montegufoni seemed to become more enormous; an infinite amount of thought and labor had been expended upon its reparation: yet my father had been singularly successful in retaining the air of forlorn grandeur, of pomp and riches in decline, which had impressed him as one of its beauties when first he saw this great building. . . ."

33. MONTOLIVETO (v.6)
Pen and black ink and gray wash over preliminary indications in black chalk. 10⅞ × 18¾ inches (277 × 476 mm.) Watermark
Inscribed: *Veduta di Montoliveto.*

Probably this is a view of the church of San Bartolomeo at Montoliveto, overlooking the southwest section of Florence.

34. VIEW OF THE ARNO RIVER FROM THE PORTA SAN FREDIANO (v.7)
Pen and black ink over preliminary indications in red chalk. 10 13/16 × 18½ inches (275 × 470 mm.). Watermark. The ruled border has been trimmed on three sides.
Inscribed: *Veduta della Pescaia d'Arno fuori della Porta à San Frediano.*

A complete view of the mill, the Mulina della Vagaloggia,

which appears in shadow in one of the views of Florence (catalogue no. 7), can be seen in this less finished drawing. The mill is located across the river from the Porta San Frediano, a fourteenth-century gate which is connected with one of the few surviving sections of the old city wall. The dome of the church which shares the name of the gate can be seen just beyond it.

35. VILLA CASTEL PULCI (v.8)
Pen and black and some brown ink, and gray wash over preliminary indications in black chalk. 11 × 18¾ inches (280 × 477 mm.)
Inscribed: *Villa di Castel Pulci del Sig:ᵣ March:ˢᵉ Riccardi.*

Like many other great Florentine houses, the Pulci met financial reverses in the early years of the fourteenth century, and their villa and lands were seized by the Cardinal Napoleone Orsini, one of their creditors. Luigi Pulci (1432–84) was a poet of some renown patronized by Cosimo, Piero and Lorenzo de' Medici. The villa is situated at Lastra a Signa, a few miles west of Florence, on a slight rise above the broad, fertile plain of the Arno. Castel Pulci was constructed about 1280, and amplified and beautified in later times. The approach through the avenue of cypresses is astoundingly similar today to Zocchi's view. In the middle of the nineteenth century Castel Pulci was purchased by the state and has been since then a hospital for the insane.

36. THE BRIDGE AT SIGNA FROM THE EAST (v.9)
Pen and black ink. 10 15/16 × 18 11/16 inches (278 × 475 mm.)
Inscribed: *Il Ponte à Signa dalla parte di Levante.*

Signa and Ponte a Signa, which lie about ten miles west of Florence on the Arno River, are typical Tuscan industrial towns. The factories line the banks of the river on either side, and the houses of the townsfolk sprawl over the hills. Signa is famous for its ceramics, and especially for the manufacture of straw hats, an important industry there since the seventeenth century. The bridge in this view connected Signa on the north bank with Ponte a Signa on the left bank. When it was first erected in the twelfth century, it provided the only crossing of the river between Florence and Pisa. It has been rebuilt many times; the present bridge was constructed following World War II.

37. THE BRIDGE AT SIGNA FROM THE WEST (V.10)

Pen and black ink. 10⅞ × 18¾ inches (276 × 476 mm.) Watermark
Inscribed: *Il Ponte à Signa dalla parte di Ponente.*

Although the riverfront of twentieth-century Ponte a Signa bears little resemblance to its eighteenth-century appearance, the church and campanile at the left of the drawing are still in existence.

38. VILLA MANCINI IN THE VICINITY OF SIGNA (V.11)

Pen and black ink. 11 × 18¾ inches (280 × 475 mm.)
Inscribed: *Villa de SS:ri Mancini vicino à Signa detta Castelletti.*

The Villa Mancini now houses an agricultural college.

39. THE CENTRAL PORT IN THE VICINITY OF PONTE A SIGNA (V.12)

Pen and black ink. 10⅞ × 18 11/16 inches (277 × 475 mm.)
Inscribed: *Veduta del Porto di mezzo vicino al Ponte à Signa.*

The large villa on the crest of the hill overlooking the river is the Villa Le Selve, another of the architect Bernardo Buontalenti's achievements. Owned successively by the Strozzi and the Salviati families, from 1611 to 1614 the villa was lent to Galileo Galilei, who occupied his time there in the study of sunspots and the lunar attraction. Another view of the villa and the church of Le Selve behind it can be seen in the drawing of the bridge at Signa from the east (catalogue no. 36).

40. THE LOWER PORT OF THE GONFOLINA (V.13)

Pen and black ink. 11 × 18¾ inches (280 × 477 mm.)
Inscribed: *Porto di Sotto nella Golfolina all' Imboccatura dell' Ombrone.*

The Arno follows a fairly direct course west from Florence until it passes under the Ponte a Signa. From there it enters the narrow, tortuous gorge excavated by the river known as the Gonfolina (Gola di Gonfolina, or Golfolina). Here at the mouth of the Ombrone River are massive rocks which are still quarried. One, similar to that in the drawing, is distinguished by the name Fairy Rock (*Masso di Fate*) because of the tiny natural grotto behind it.

41. THE COUNTRYSIDE ALONG THE ARNO IN THE GONFOLINA GORGE (V.14)

Pen and black ink, and gray wash. 11 × 18⅝ inches (280 × 475 mm.)
Inscribed: *Veduta di Paese sul corso del Fiume Arno nella Golfolina, e della R: Villa d'Artimino in lontananza.*

The Villa Artimino (catalogue no. 49) is in the distance.

42. THE ARNO RIVER IN THE GRUMAGGIO
REGION (V 15)

Pen and black ink, and gray wash. 10⅞ × 18⅝ inches (277 × 474 mm.)
Watermark
Inscribed: *Veduta sul Fiume Arno dalla parte di Grumaggio.*

From the rocky terrain it is clear that the site of this drawing
is not far from that of the preceding drawing in the series,
but present-day guidebooks do not designate the area by
this name.

43. THE COUNTRYSIDE ALONG THE ARNO
RIVER IN THE GONFOLINA GORGE (V.16)

Pen and black ink. 11 1/16 × 18¾ inches (280 × 476 mm.)
Inscribed: *Veduta di Paese sul Fiume Arno nella Golfolina.*

The spirit of this pastoral scene recalls the landscapes of
Claude Lorrain of a century before.

44. VILLA AMBROGIANA (V.17)

Pen and black ink. 11 × 18 11/16 inches (280 × 474 mm.)
Inscribed: *La Real Villa dell' Ambrogiana.*

Ferdinando de' Medici bought the property for Ambrogiana
in 1587. It is at Montelupo, which is located west of Florence at the junction of the Arno and Pesa rivers. The iden-
tity of the architect has not been precisely established, but
Buontalenti may have had a hand in designing the majestic
structure. Ferdinand was apparently in accord with the following contemporary description of it, for he used it as his
preferred hunting lodge: "The form is square with four
towers rising at angles after the fashion of a strong castle,
with courtyard adorned with fountains and outside other
fountains and shady avenues of plane trees, and pergolas,

and gardens, and woods, and grottoes, and other delights
and it serves as a villa and is in the country fit for the hunt of
wild beasts." By Zocchi's time the pergolas and some of the
gardens had succumbed to the additions of chapels, stables,
and tennis courts installed by later Medici princes. It is now
a hospital for the criminally insane.

45. CASTELFIORENTINO (V.18)

Pen and black ink, and gray wash. 11 × 18⅝ inches (280 × 472 mm.)
Watermark
Inscribed: *Veduta di Castel Fiorentino.*

Located about nineteen miles southwest of Florence on the
Elsa River, the city of Castelfiorentino is the center of the most
fertile region of Tuscany. It dates from Roman times, and
was originally called Castel Timignano. The present name
was first used in the twelfth century when the city fell under
the domination of the Florentines, who used it as a bulwark
of defense against Siena. Consequently, Castelfiorentino
suffered the fate of becoming a battleground for the frequent
clashes between the two communes. Today the city divides
into a lively modern section on the plain overlooked by the
historical area on the steep hill.

46. LA CECINA (V.19)

Pen and black ink, and gray wash. 11 × 18⅝ inches (279 × 472 mm.)
Inscribed: *La Cecina di S. Ecc:ᶻᵃ il Sig:ʳ Sen:ʳᵉ Mar:ˢᵉ Carlo Ginori.*

The owner of this complex of buildings was Carlo Ginori,
who founded the celebrated porcelain industry, still flour-
ishing today, in 1735, at about the same time the porcelain
factories at Meissen, Vienna, and Sèvres were beginning to
produce. The firm, now Richard-Ginori, is located in Sesto

Fiorentino, a small community a few miles northwest of Florence. Zocchi's drawing, however, is not a rendition of the porcelain manufactory, but another Ginori establishment. Francis II of Lorrain permitted Ginori to lease some property which had formerly belonged to the Medici at Cécina, in the Tuscan swamps south of Livorno on the west coast where the Cécina River flows into the sea. According to one account, the Marchese Ginori operated a dairy farm here, and from the evidence of the drawing, a boatyard as well. Although he was active in pressing forward the project of reclaiming the land in the area, eventually Francis II's dispensation was rescinded, and the tenancy was taken over by some forty farmers.

47. VILLA CORSI AT SESTO (v.20)

Pen and black ink. 10⅞ × 18½ inches (278 × 471 mm.) Watermark
Inscribed: *Villa di Sesto delli SS:ri Marchesi Corsi.*

The main façade of this villa (now usually called the Villa Corsi-Salviati) lines the side of a busy street in Sesto, and it comes as a surprise to step into the extensive gardens behind it shown in Zocchi's view. The villa is situated in the middle of a wide plain, and was a simple country house when it was acquired by Jacopo Corsi in 1502. Although additions were made before 1738, the drawing shows it shortly after that year, as it was then that the Corsi added the baroque façade and arranged the garden pools, parterres, paths, and woods (*bosco*) almost as we see them now. By the middle of the nineteenth century, the villa was famous for its flowers and semi-exotic plants. The present owners have studiously retained the garden's eighteenth-century character.

48. VILLA POGGIO A CAIANO (v.21)

Pen and black ink over preliminary indications in black chalk.
10⅞ × 18⅝ inches (275 × 474 mm.) Watermark
Inscribed: *La Real Villa del Poggio à Caiano.*

Giuliano da San Gallo was employed about 1480 by Lorenzo il Magnifico to rebuild the villa at Poggio a Caiano. Lorenzo's son Giovanni (later Pope Leo X) carried on the project, adding the beautiful central loggia with its Della Robbia frieze, and the pediment. Frescoes by Filippino Lippi, Andrea del Sarto, Pontormo, and Franciabigio adorned the interior. The villa played an important part in the lives of the Medici. As it was a convenient staging point west of the city, it was often used for the reception of important guests before they made a ceremonial entrance into the city, and many prospective brides met their Medici bridegrooms for the first time at Poggio a Caiano. Zocchi's choice of depicting the side of the villa with the Ombrone River in the foreground is rather unusual, but it did give him an opportunity to exploit the rural setting fully. The villa is now owned by the state and is open as a museum.

49. VILLA ARTIMINO (v.22)

Pen and black ink over preliminary indications in black chalk.
11 × 18½ inches (278 × 468 mm.)
Inscribed: *La Reale Villa d'Artimino.*

The story goes that Ferdinando I, Grand Duke of Tuscany, finding himself while hunting one day above the village of Artimino, commissioned Bernardo Buontalenti to build a palace for him on that very spot. The villa stands on the crest of a high hill which slopes down to the northern bank of the Arno. Spreading before it to the east, north, and southeast is a magnificent panorama, in the midst of which

is Signa, and about eight miles beyond Signa, Florence. Poggio a Caiano is visible about three miles to the north. Buontalenti's elegant building of imposing dimensions and smooth, immaculately white exterior appears almost surprising in the midst of the rustic situation. Perhaps because the ornament is largely confined to the loggia and the interior, Artimino is very well preserved. It remained in the hands of the rulers of Tuscany until 1782 when it was sold by Pierre Leopold of Lorraine. It is still privately owned.

50. VILLA MAGIA (v.23)

Pen and black ink over preliminary indications in black chalk.
11 × 18¾ inches (278 × 476 mm.)
Inscribed: *Villa della Magia del Sig:ʳ Pandolfo Attavanti.*

The Villa Magia is in the village of Quarrata in a rural area west of Florence. It was acquired by Francesco I de' Medici in 1583. Who the architect was who reconstructed the villa for him is not known, although Buontalenti may have as-

sisted in the project. It is an unpretentious, informal, rambling structure, irregular in plan and elevation. From Zocchi's drawing, it appears to have been in the eighteenth century the comfortable family residence it still is today.

51. VILLA BARONE (v.24)

Pen and black ink over preliminary indications in black chalk.
11 × 18¾ inches (280 × 475 mm.)
Inscribed: *Villa del Barone delli SS:ʳⁱ Marchesi Tempi.*

Located against a back-drop of hills, the Villa Barone is just north of the city of Montemurlo between Prato and Pistoia. It now serves as a hospital.

52. VILLA CERRETO (v.25)

Pen and black ink over preliminary indications in black chalk.
10⅞ × 18½ inches (277 × 470 mm.) Watermark
Inscribed: *La Real Villa di Cerreto.*

Mounted at the peak of the hill-town of Cerreto Guidi, the severely simple, almost forbidding villa is reached by pre-

cipitous ramps, which zig-zag up the slope. This grandiose approach, the "Ponti Medicei," was designed by Bernardo Buontalenti. The climber is rewarded at the summit by a breathtaking view of the vineyard-covered plains below. The parochial church of San Leonardo at the left of the drawing has been considerably altered since Zocchi's time. The villa, commonly known as the Villa Medicea, is privately owned, but is closed.

53. VILLA ROSPIGLIOSI (v.26)

Pen and black ink over preliminary indications in black chalk. $10\frac{15}{16} \times 18\frac{1}{2}$ inches (278 × 470 mm.) The artist has made a correction in the drawing by the addition of paper in the upper right corner.
Inscribed: *Veduta della Villa di Lamporecchio di S.E.ᶻᵃ il Sʳ Duca Rospigliosi.*

The cultivated Duke of Rospigliosi, who became Pope Clement IX in 1667, was Gian Lorenzo Bernini's devoted friend and patron. Although it is now generally agreed that the design for Clement IX's country villa in Lamporecchio (not far from Pistoia in the Albani mountains) was not made by the master himself, but by his assistant, Mattia de' Rossi, it is not entirely impossible that Rossi based his plan on a Bernini sketch. The villa was commissioned in 1669, the year of the Pope's death. Perhaps for this reason it was never completed and was nicknamed *Spicchio* (segment). The beautifully proportioned chapel has also been associated with Bernini's name. The villa and its chapel are privately owned.

54. VILLA BELLAVISTA (v.27)

Pen and black ink. $10\frac{3}{4} \times 18\frac{5}{8}$ inches (275 × 473 mm.) Watermark
Inscribed: *Villa di Bella Vista del S: Mar: Francesco Ferroni.*

Bellavista was constructed near Pescia in 1672 for the Marchese Ferroni by Antonio Ferri, who also worked on the Villa Corsini (catalogue no. 57) and Lapeggi (catalogue no. 77). It is a splendid edifice with a sumptuously ornamented entrance. The villa is now a home for firemen and their orphaned children.

55. THE ASCENT TO THE CAPUCHIN CHURCH AND MONASTERY (v.28)

Pen and black ink, and gray wash over preliminary indications in black chalk. $10\frac{15}{16} \times 18\frac{5}{8}$ inches (277 × 473 mm.) Watermark
Inscribed: *Salita alla Chiesa, e Convento de P. P. Cappuccini de Montughi.*

The artist may have paused to do this drawing *en route* to the top of the hill from which he drew the panoramic scene which is the first in the series of views of Florence. The monastery to which he was making his way was built in the thirteenth century for the Umiliati order, the famous wool manufacturers. After the suppression of the order by the Medici, it passed to the Osservanti, then to the Capuchin order in 1572. The monastery once housed a pharmacy and a printing establishment as well as the woolen factory.

56. VILLA GERINI AT MONTUGHI (v.29)

Pen and black ink. $11 \times 18\frac{7}{8}$ inches (280 × 478 mm.)
Inscribed: *Villa di Montughi delli SS:ʳⁱ Marchesi Gerini.*

Zocchi's series of the views of villas includes three which were owned by his patron, Andrea Gerini. This was the closest to the city; in fact, Florence has now grown around it. Although a seminary is located on the site of the villa, little or nothing remains of the original building.

57. VILLA CORSINI (v.30)

Pen and black ink. $10^7/_8 \times 18\,^7/_{16}$ inches (276×468 mm.) Watermark
Inscribed: *Villa di Castello di S. E. il Sig.^{r} Principe Corsini.*

The name of Rinieri has been associated with this villa since 1460 when that family acquired it from the Strozzi, but there has been a long succession of well-known owners. One of the most colorful was the Englishman Robert Dudley, Duke of Northumberland, who died at the villa in 1649. He was an explorer, engineer, and author who was employed by Cosimo II de' Medici to drain the marshes behind Livorno and build a port there. The Corsini family acquired the villa in 1687. The beautifully preserved seventeenth-century façade was designed by Antonio Ferri; the fountains and gardens are attributed to Tribolo. The entrance gate and walls still stand, but the green for *bocce* ball has been sacrificed to the widening of the road. Villa Petraia, also in the village of Castello, is now obscured from view although it appears to be nearby in the drawing. The villa is at present privately owned, but it is hoped that it will soon be acquired by the state and its house and gardens preserved as an historic site.

58. VILLA CAREGGI (v.31)

Pen and black ink, and gray wash. $11 \times 18\,^9/_{16}$ inches (280×471 mm.)
Inscribed: *La Real Villa di Careggi.*

The humanistic conception of the villa as a place of repose and cultivation of the arts was nowhere so well realized as at Careggi. It was the first of the Medici country houses, converted by Michelozzo in 1434 from an old castellated house into a palace with courtyard, loggias, and gardens, which were in time adorned with statuary and exotic plants. Cosimo il Vecchio established at Careggi a Platonic Academy, which during his grandson Lorenzo's lifetime became the most famous intellectual center of the world. The scholar Marsilio Ficino was given a house on the grounds. After the death of Lorenzo at Careggi, the Medici were expelled, and the villa was looted and burned. It was restored for the later Medici dukes by Pontormo and Bronzino, and is now part of a hospital.

59. VILLA CASTELLO (v.32)

Pen and black ink. $10^7/_8 \times 18^3/_4$ inches (275×475 mm.)
Inscribed: *La Real Villa di Castello.*

The road in front of the Villa Corsini leads directly to the Villa Castello, a long, low villa on a gentle incline above the highway from Florence to Sesto. The house had been Medici property for a century when in 1540 Cosimo I commissioned Tribolo to improve the gardens. By tradition, the original plan for this work was so vast that neither Tribolo nor his successor Buontalenti was able to realize all the fountains, statues, grottoes, secret gardens, and labyrinths. Nevertheless, Vasari described it as the most rich, magnificent, and ornamental garden in Europe. The villa has been the property of the state since 1919 and had until recently been used as a school; it is now the new seat of the Accademia della Crusca.

60. VILLA PETRAIA (v.33)

Pen and black ink. $11 \times 18^3/_4$ inches (280×477 mm.) Watermark
Inscribed: *La Real Villa della Petraia.*

This villa in Castello is celebrated for the gallant defense made in 1364 by its first owners, the Brunelleschi, against the Pisans and their German and English allies under Sir John Hawkwood. In 1561, Bernardo Buontalenti was hired by the Medici, who had by then acquired it, to transform the primitive castle into a fashionable villa. Eventually, it became the favored residence of Victor Emmanuel II and the Countess Mirafiori. The gardens here were also laid out by Tribolo; the lovely fountain by Giovanni da Bologna with the woman wringing out her long hair was moved here in the eighteenth century from the Villa Castello. In 1919, Petraia became state property, and is now open to the public.

61. VILLA PRATOLINO (v.34)

Pen and brown ink, brown and some gray wash over preliminary indications in black chalk. 11 × 18½ inches (280 × 470 mm.)
Inscribed: *La Reale Villa di Pratolino.*

Francesco de' Medici purchased the land for Pratolino in an area about six miles north of Florence in 1569, and obtained the services of Buontalenti as architect. By 1579 it was suitably finished to be used as a retreat. John Evelyn, the English diarist, who visited it in 1645, reported: "The house is square with four pavilions, with a fair platform about it, balustred with stone, situate in a large meadow . . . . The whole place seems consecrated to pleasure and summer retirement." It was in the garden that Buontalenti exploited the full scope of his artistic and mechanical genius, as it was filled with aquatic surprises, mysterious fountains, and hidden jets of water which delighted and harassed the innocent visitor. Ferdinando de' Medici, Cosimo III's son, adored Pratolino and commissioned Antonio Ferri to build a theatre in the third story where operas by Scarlatti were performed. When Ferdinando died in 1737, the theatre was closed forever, and the villa began to deteriorate. In 1814, the building was demolished and the grounds transformed into an English park. A few remnants of the garden sculpture, among them Giovanni da Bologna's colossal *Appenino*, remain.

62. THE BRIDGE AT SAN PIERO A SIEVE (v.35)

Pen and black ink. 11 × 18⅝ inches (278 × 472 mm.)
Inscribed: *Veduta del Ponte à S: Piero à Sieve.*

The most prominent feature of the small farming town of San Piero a Sieve is the imposing Fort of San Martino which lies on the steep slope above the bridge in the midst of a lovely pine forest. The fort was designed by Bernardo Buontalenti for the Medici in 1571. In the drawing, the artist, his large sketchbook in hand, is apparently pointing to its crenelated walls.

63. VILLA CAFAGGIOLO (v.36)

Pen and black ink. 11 × 18 9/16 inches (280 × 472 mm.) Watermark
Inscribed: *La Real Villa di Cafaggiolo.*

Vasari records that Cafaggiolo was built by Cosimo de' Medici with the advice and design of Michelozzo, "in the guise of a fortress with ditches surrounding; and he laid out the farms, the streets, the gardens, and the fountains with woods round about, fowling places, and other things much esteemed in villas." This substantial structure is located north of Florence above the Sieve River. Although its moats, gardens, and one of its towers have disappeared, it is still a formidable example of fifteenth-century architecture. The villa is now a Trappist monastery.

64. VILLA LE MASCHERE (v.37)

Pen and black ink. 11 × 18⅝ inches (278 × 473 mm.) Watermark
Inscribed: *Villa delli SS:ri Marchesi Gerini detta le Maschere.*

Still owned by a descendant of Andrea Gerini, the villa is remarkably unchanged in appearance after two centuries, except for the transposition of the clock and the coat of arms on the façade. Ottavio Gerini acquired Le Maschere in 1611, and it was restyled in the eighteenth century when it was owned by Andrea. It is located north of Florence on the road to Bologna near Barberini di Mugello.

later, when it was owned by the Earl of Crawford, Queen Victoria stayed here on her visits to Florence. In the 1920's, the owner was an American, James Ellsworth, father of the explorer. Today the villa is once more the property of a Florentine family.

65. VILLA GERINI AT RONTA (v.38)
Pen and black ink over preliminary indications in black chalk.
11 × 18½ inches (280 × 470 mm.) Watermark
Inscribed: *Villa de. SS:ri Marchesi Gerini à Ronta.*

There seems little doubt that this, the least pretentious of the Gerini houses in the series, was actually the Gerini farm. Ronta, on the Elsa River northeast of Florence, is still an agricultural village of less than a thousand inhabitants frequented by travelers on a country holiday.

66. VILLA PALMIERI (v.39)
Pen and black ink. 11 × 18 9/16 inches (278 × 471 mm.)
Inscribed: *Tre Visi Villa de SS:ri Palmieri al principio della Salita di Fiesole.*

On the slope below San Domenico in Fiesole stands the Villa Palmieri, immortalized by Boccaccio in the *Decameron*. The stately mansion and its extensive grounds represent a gradual evolution of ideas by successive owners, but Boccaccio's description can still be applied: "The young people were so enraptured with the garden and its arrangement of plants, the fountain and the streamlets flowing from it, that they agreed if Paradise were possible on earth it would not be conceivable except in the shape of this beautiful place." The name derives from the distinguished writer Matteo Palmieri who bought the villa in 1454. A great many years

67. PONTE ALLA BADIA (v.40)
Pen and black ink. 11 × 18½ inches (278 × 470 mm.) Watermark
Inscribed: *Veduta del Ponte alla Badia.*

Modern photographs bear witness to the fact that until World War II this picturesque quarter of Fiesole in the suburbs of Florence survived almost intact from the eighteenth century. It is now much changed. The Badia nearby is considered to be one of the finest examples of fifteenth-century Florentine architecture.

68. VILLA SALVIATI (v.41)
Pen and black ink over preliminary indications in black chalk.
10⅞ × 18¾ inches (277 × 475 mm.)
Inscribed: *Villa del Ponte alla Badia di S. E.za il Sig:r Duca Salviati.*

In spite of the inevitable alterations of time and wear, like Cafaggiolo this basically thirteenth-century villa still retains its fortress-like appearance. Large trees now fill the terraces which command a fine view of Fiesole and Florence. The villa was acquired in 1469 by the Salviati family, who did not relinquish its ownership until the eighteenth century. It is now privately owned. The inner court is ornamented with a series of large terra-cotta medallions made by Jacopo Rustici in the early sixteenth century.

69. VILLA GUADAGNI (v.42)

Pen and black ink, and gray wash over preliminary indications in black chalk. 11 × 18½ inches (280 × 470 mm.) Watermark
Inscribed: *Villa della Luna delli SS:ri March:si Guadagni.*

This villa in the Della Luna section of Fiesole came into the hands of the Guadagni family at the end of the sixteenth century. It had been built a hundred years earlier from designs of Giuliano da San Gallo, but was enlarged and refurbished by its new owners. During World War I it served as a hospital.

70. VILLA BARTOLINI (v.43)

Pen and black ink, and gray wash. 11 1/16 × 18⅞ inches (282 × 478 mm.) Watermark. The artist has corrected a section at the right of the drawing by adding paper.
Inscribed: *Villa del Sig:r Marchese Bartolini à Rovezzano.*

Baccio d'Agnolo, who built the Bartolini-Salimbeni family a handsome city palace on the Piazza Santa Trinita (catalogue no. 16), reconstructed for them also this villa in Rovezzano, a short distance southeast of the city. The villa remained in the family's possession until the nineteenth century. One of its subsequent owners was the Baroness Fiorella Favard, friend of Napoleon III, for whom it is frequently called the Villa Favard. The façade was restored in the seventeenth century by Giuseppe Parigi. A charitable order now maintains the villa as the "Casa Serena."

71. VILLA LORETINO (v.44)

Pen and black ink. 11 × 18⅞ inches (280 × 478 mm.)
Inscribed: *Veduta di Paese dalla Villa di Loretino.*

Nineteenth-century additions have changed the appearance of the villa, of which only a corner is visible in the drawing, but its chapel dedicated to the Madonna of Loreto, from which the name derives, is intact. The site, near Settignano, was first used in the thirteenth century for a palace of the Tebaldini family who had departed permanently from Florence for political reasons. After passing through several hands, it was acquired early in the fifteenth century by Francesco Franceschi. He is credited with the construction of the chapel, the reconstruction of the villa, and the introduction into Tuscany by transporting five cuttings from Spanish vines of the cultivation of a superior wine called Leatico. The villa is privately owned.

72. THE ENTRANCE TO THE VILLA GAMBERAIA (v.45)

Pen and black ink. 11 1/16 × 18⅞ inches (282 × 480 mm.)
Inscribed: *Veduta dell' ingresso alla Villa di Gamberaia del Sig:r Marchese Capponi.*

As in the eighteenth century, the entrance to the present Villa Gamberaia leads from a walled road which tunnels under one end of the garden.

73. LANDSCAPE IN THE VICINITY OF GAMBERAIA (v.46)

Pen and black ink. 11 1/16 × 18 13/16 inches (280 × 478 mm.)
Inscribed: *Veduta di Campagna vicino à Gamberaia.*

Visiting Settignano today, it is easy to understand why Zocchi included in the series the two pastoral scenes from the vicinity of Gamberaia. Even this road-side shrine remains amidst the unspoiled rural beauty.

74. VILLA GAMBERAIA (v.47)

Pen and black ink, 10 15/16 × 18 3/4 inches (278 × 476 mm.)
Inscribed: *Villa di Gamberaia del Sig:ʳ Marchese Scipione Capponi.*

Although the villa itself was destroyed during World War II,
it has been completely rebuilt by the present owners. The
gardens, considered to be the most beautiful small gardens
in Tuscany, have also been restored. The Capponi family
acquired the property in Settignano in 1717, and it is likely
that the garden assumed its present form at this time. It is
known that it was then that the bowling green was laid out,
cypresses planted, reflecting pools installed, and the statues
put in place. Zocchi's view from the side emphasizes the
building rather than its now more famous gardens.

75. VILLA LE FALLE (v.48)

Pen and black ink. 11 × 18 1/2 inches (279 × 470 mm.)
Inscribed: *Villa delle Falle de SS:ʳⁱ Guadagni dall' Opera.*

Superb lanes of cypresses still lead to the Villa Le Falle. At
one time the villa belonged to the Pazzi family, prominent
bankers and rivals of the Medici. Following the ill-starred
Pazzi Conspiracy in 1478, during which Giuliano de' Medici was murdered in the Cathedral, Le Falle was confiscated
along with other Pazzi properties. The turreted twelfth-
century castle was reconstructed by Gherardo Silvani for
the Guadagni family, who acquired it in 1599. Mindful of
the fine view of the surrounding hills and plains, and the
Arno below, Silvani's alterations included the expansion of
the windows of the loggia, and the addition of a terrace en-
circling the entire building. The villa is located near Com-
piobbi, east of Florence. It is privately owned, and has recently been reconstructed to conform to its eighteenth-
century appearance.

76. VILLA LA TANA (v.49)

Pen and brown ink, and brown wash. 11 × 18 3/4 inches (279 × 475
mm.)
Inscribed: *La Tana Villa de SS:ʳⁱ Baroni Ricasoli.*

The pale ink of the drawing does not do justice to the ele-
gance of this villa of golden stucco trimmed in warm
brown. The sixteenth-century building in which the ill-fated
Bianca Cappella once lived was reconstructed in the seventeenth century for the Baron Ricasoli, whose coat of arms
ornaments the façade, and was amplified further by later
owners. It is now one of the most beautifully preserved and
tended of the Tuscan villas, with a magnificent view of Florence from its terrace. The central approach shown in Zoc-

chi's view was never possible as the land drops off sharply at the edge of the terrace a short distance in front of the double staircase; the extensive gardens range behind and at the side of the building. The villa is in Candeli, not far south of the city, and is privately owned.

77. VILLA LAPEGGI (v.50)
Pen and black ink. 11 × 18 9/16 inches (280 × 472 mm.)
Inscribed: *La Reale Villa di Lappeggi.*

Francesco de' Medici acquired Lapeggi (about six miles southeast of Florence) in 1569 from the Ricasoli. When the Cardinal Francesco Maria de' Medici inherited it more than a century later, it was still a modest country house. The cardinal was inspired by the wonders of Pratolino, and hired Antonio Ferri to make the improvements at Lapeggi. The story goes that the architect gave the cardinal two choices: construction that would be permanent or decoration that would last fifteen or twenty years. The cardinal chose the less expensive, and after his death in 1711, the villa began to crumble away. Time and earthquakes finished the task.

PLATES

Scelta
di XXIV. Vedute delle principali
Contrade, Piazze, Chiese, e Palazzi
della Città di Firenze
Dedicata
Alla Sacra, Reale, Apostolica
Maestà di
Maria Teresa
Regina d'Ungheria,
e di Boemia,
Arciduchessa d'Austria,
e Granduchessa
di Toscana, &c. &c. &c.

Questo Frontespizio dato ora in luce per la prima volta, è preso
dalla Pittura originale à fresco fatta dal Mannozzi detto Giovanni
da San Giovanni nel Prospetto di una Casa posta in Firenze in faccia
alla Porta Romana.

2. TITLE PAGE: VIEWS OF FLORENCE

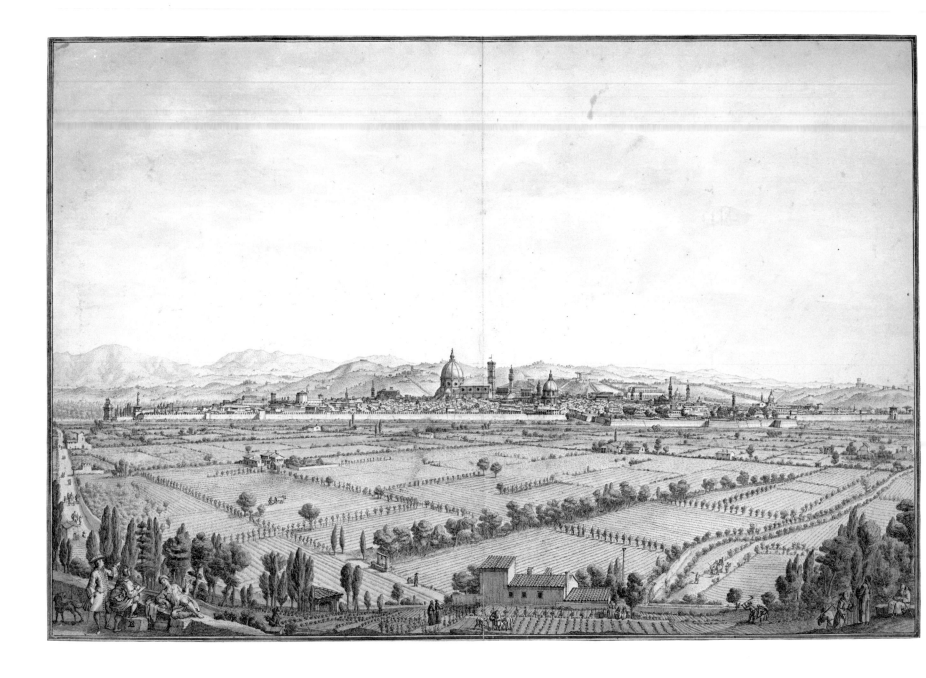

3. VIEW OF FLORENCE FROM THE CAPUCHIN MONASTERY IN MONTUGHI

4. THE PITTI PALACE

5. VIEW ALONG THE ARNO RIVER FROM THE PORTA ALLA CROCE

6. VIEW ALONG THE ARNO RIVER FROM THE PORTA A SAN NICCOLÒ

7. VIEW ALONG THE ARNO RIVER FROM THE VAGA LOGGIA

8. THE ARNO RIVER AND THE PONTE SANTA TRINITA

9. THE ARNO RIVER FROM THE RUCELLAI TERRACE

IO.   THE CORSINI PALACE ON THE ARNO RIVER

II. THE CHURCH AND PIAZZA OGNISSANTI

12. THE STROZZI PALACE, THE CENTAURO, AND THE STREET LEADING TO SANTA MARIA NOVELLA

13.   CHURCH OF SAN MICHELE BERTELDE

14. THE CORSI AND VIVIANI PALACES

15. THE STROZZI PALACE AND THE STREET LEADING TO THE PONTE SANTA TRINITA

16. THE PIAZZA SANTA TRINITA

17. THE PIAZZA SANTISSIMA ANNUNZIATA

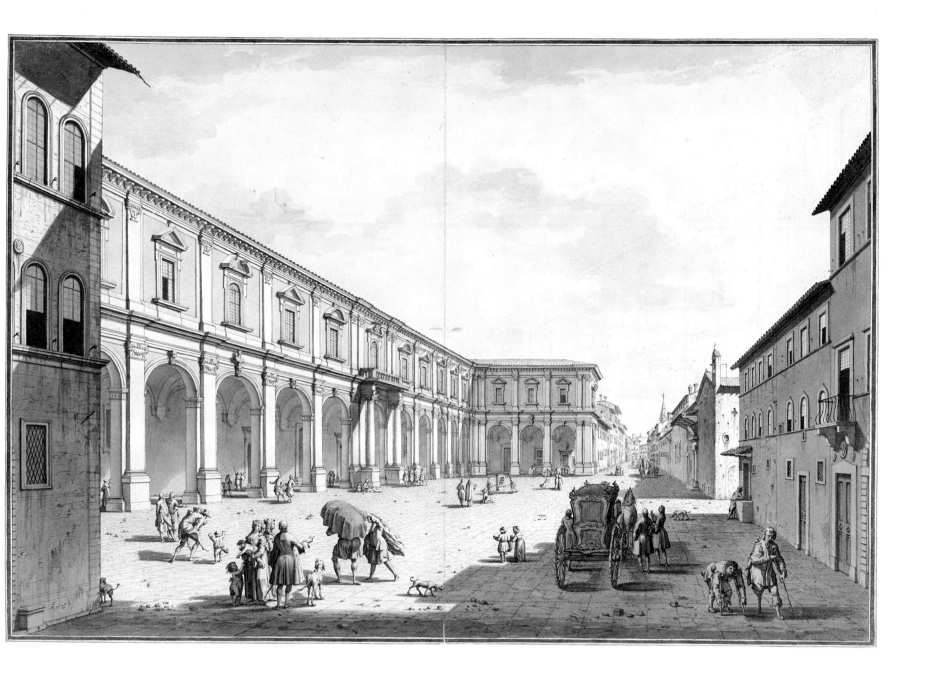

18. THE HOSPITAL AND PIAZZA OF SANTA MARIA NUOVA

19. CHURCH AND PIAZZA SAN PIER MAGGIORE

20. THE BADIA FIORENTINA AND THE PALAZZO DEL PODESTÀ

21. THE CHURCH OF SAN GIOVANNINO AND THE RICCARDI PALACE

22. THE UFFIZI FROM THE LOGGIA NEAR THE ARNO RIVER

23. THE CATHEDRAL AND BAPTISTERY DURING THE PROCESSION OF CORPUS DOMINI

24.   THE CHURCH AND PIAZZA OF SANTA MARIA NOVELLA DURING THE CHARIOT RACE

25.   THE PIAZZA DELLA SIGNORIA DURING THE FESTIVAL OF HOMAGE

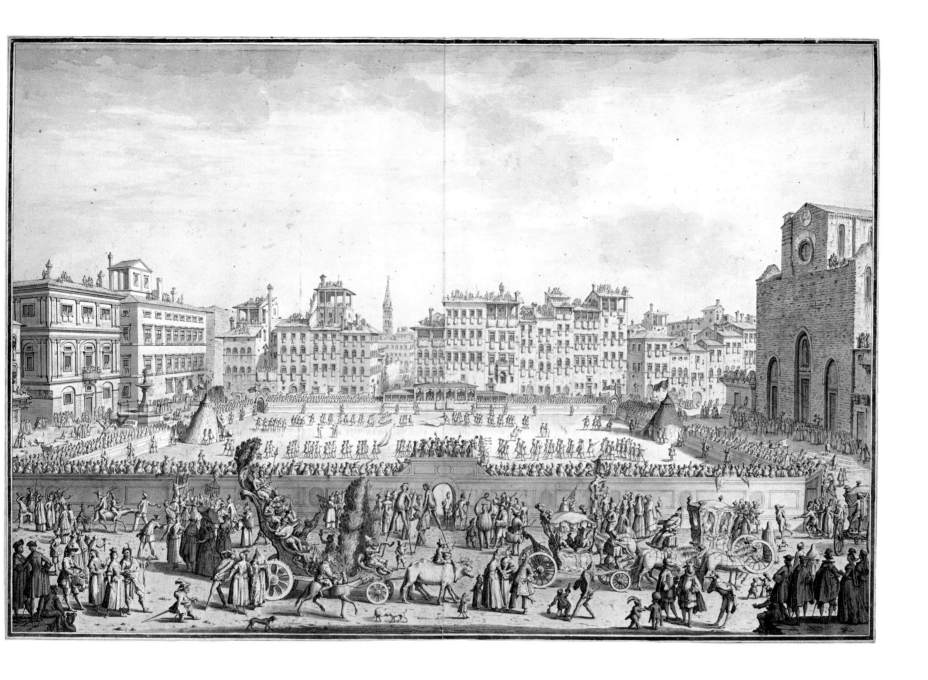

26. THE CHURCH AND PIAZZA OF SANTA CROCE

VEDVTE
DI·VILLE, E·LVOGHI
DELLA·TOSCANA.
AN·MDCCXXXXIV.

27. TITLE PAGE: VIEWS OF VILLAS AND SITES IN TUSCANY

28. VILLA POGGIO IMPERIALE

29. LA PACE

30. VILLA RICCI AT POZZOLATICO

31. VILLA I COLLAZZI

32.   CASTLE OF MONTEGUFONI

33. MONTOLIVETO

34. VIEW OF THE ARNO RIVER FROM THE PORTA SAN FREDIANO

35. VILLA CASTEL PULCI

36. THE BRIDGE AT SIGNA FROM THE EAST

37. THE BRIDGE AT SIGNA FROM THE WEST

38. VILLA MANCINI IN THE VICINITY OF SIGNA

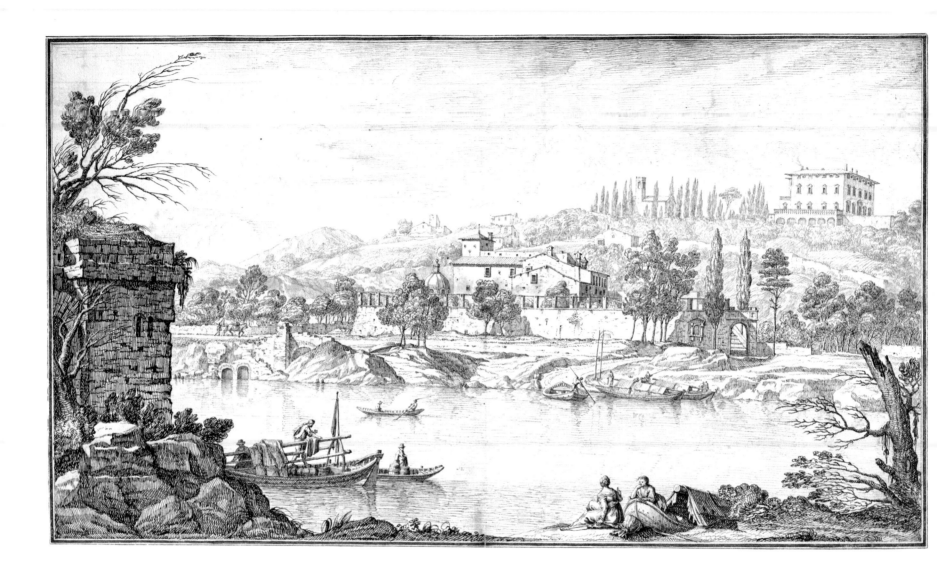

39.   THE CENTRAL PORT IN THE VICINITY OF PONTE A SIGNA

40. THE LOWER PORT OF THE GONFOLINA

41. THE COUNTRYSIDE ALONG THE ARNO IN THE GONFOLINA GORGE

42. THE ARNO RIVER IN THE GRUMAGGIO REGION

43. THE COUNTRYSIDE ALONG THE ARNO RIVER IN THE GONFOLINA GORGE

44. VILLA AMBROGIANA

45. CASTELFIORENTINO

46. LA CECINA

47. VILLA CORSI AT SESTO

48. VILLA POGGIO A CAIANO

49. VILLA ARTIMINO

50.　VILLA MAGIA

51. VILLA BARONE

52. VILLA CERRETO

53. VILLA ROSPIGLIOSI

54. VILLA BELLAVISTA

55. THE ASCENT TO THE CAPUCHIN CHURCH AND MONASTERY

56. VILLA GERINI AT MONTUGHI

57. VILLA CORSINI

58. VILLA CAREGGI

59. VILLA CASTELLO

60. VILLA PETRAIA

61. VILLA PRATOLINO

62. THE BRIDGE AT SAN PIERO A SIEVE

63. VILLA CAFAGGIOLO

64. VILLA LE MASCHERE

65. VILLA GERINI AT RONTA

66. VILLA PALMIERI

67. PONTE ALLA BADIA

68. VILLA SALVIATI

69. VILLA GUADAGNI

70. VILLA BARTOLINI

71. VILLA LORETINO

72. THE ENTRANCE TO THE VILLA GAMBERAIA

73. LANDSCAPE IN THE VICINITY OF GAMBERAIA

74. VILLA GAMBERAIA

75. VILLA LE FALLE

76. VILLA LA TANA

77. VILLA LAPEGGI

LOCATION MAPS

AND

INDEX OF DRAWINGS

SITE MAP OF TUSCANY

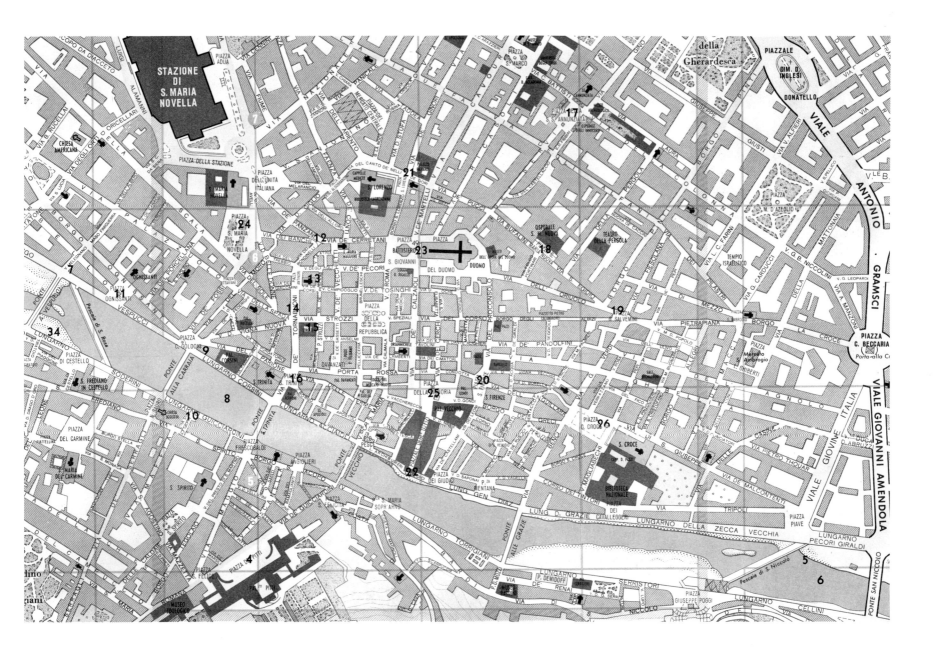

SITE MAP OF FLORENCE

INDEX